Chefs Jo

The Ultimate Collection of Chef Jokes

Published by Glowworm Press
7 Nuffield Way
Abingdon OX14 1RL
By Chester Croker

Jokes for Chefs

These tasty jokes for chefs will make you giggle. Some of them are old, some of them are freshly made, and some are simply re-heated, to create a tasty collection of the very best chef jokes and puns around.

We hope you enjoy these funny chef gags which are guaranteed to get you laughing.

FOREWORD

When I was asked to write a foreword to this book I was thrilled.

That is until I was told that I was the last resort by the author, Chester Croker, and that everyone else he had approached had said they couldn't do it!

I have known Chester for a number of years and his ability to create funny jokes is absolutely incredible. He is quick witted and an expert at crafting clever puns and amusing gags and I feel he is the ideal man to put together a joke book about our profession.

He will be glad you have bought this book, as he has an expensive lifestyle to maintain.

Enjoy!

Chris P. Bacon

Table of Contents

Chapter 1: Chef Jokes

If you're looking for funny chef jokes you've certainly come to the right place.

We've got some great one-liners to start with, plenty of quick fire questions and answers themed gags, some story led jokes and as a bonus some corny and cheesy pick-up lines for chefs.

This mixture of chef jokes will prove that chefs have a good sense of humor and we do hope you enjoy our collection of the very best chef jokes and puns around.

Chapter 2: One Liner Chef Jokes

Guess what happened when the chef found a daddy long legs in the salad. It became a daddy short legs.

Did you hear about the cannibal chef who got disciplined by his boss for buttering up the diners.

Chef tells off one of his staff "Why didn't you make all the food on that long order?" and he got this reply "Because I m a short order cook."

Waiter: "Chef, this soup is spoiled."

Chef "Who told you?"

Waiter: "A little swallow."

Customer: “A tray of sushi, please.”

Chef: "Is that to eat or to post photos of on Instagram?"

Waiter: If you know the food here is so lousy, why do you keep coming back?

Customer: It reminds me of my ex-wife's cooking.

"Chef, Is there soup on the menu tonight?"

"No, I wiped it all off."

Customer: Chef, This omelette is inedible.

Chef: We have been making omelettes since you were born.

Customer: Then why the hell are they not served until now?

I have never been in love. But I imagine it would be something like the feeling you get when you have an evening in a kitchen when everything goes exactly to plan.

The chef instructs
the head waiter,
"Can you please
push the soup of the
day. It's a week
old."

Customer: “My plate is wet.”

Waiter “Chef says that’s not wet, sit - that's the soup."

One for the kids - What kind of lettuce did they serve on The Titanic? *Iceberg*.

Customer: Excuse me, but there is a wedding ring in my soup.

Waiter: It must belong to the chef; let me know if you also find his finger.

In Hungary there is a restaurant where the waiter gives you three dice along with your bill. If you roll three sixes then the meal is on the house.

Wouldn't it be great to have a smoke detector that shuts off when you yell at it "I'm just cooking."

I entered what I ate today into my new fitness app and it just sent an ambulance to my house.

Chef's Top Tip: When baking dog biscuits, be sure to use collie flour.

Chef's words of wisdom: Cook a man a fish, and you feed him for a day. Teach him how to fish, and you get rid of him for the entire weekend.

One for the kiddies:- Why was the chef embarrassed? He saw the salad dressing.

Definition of a top chef:-

A cook who knows how to swear in French.

My friend's bakery burned down last night. His business is now toast.

A chef friend of mine gave me some great advice, saying I should put something away for a rainy day. I’ve gone for an umbrella.

Customer: “Waiter, waiter. There's a spider in my salad.”

Waiter: “Yes sir, the chef's using Webb lettuces today.”

The chef flew into a rage at his new waiter. "Didn't I tell you to notice when the soup boiled over?" "I did," said the waiter, "It was 8:30 pm."

Did you hear about
the restaurant on
the moon?

Great food but very
little atmosphere.

The chef cooks his eggs on the golf course - because he wanted them par-boiled.

The waiter tells his chef that a customer has complained that there is dirt in his soup. The waiter asks what could mean? To which the chef replies "If he wants his fortune told, he should go to a fortune teller."

I don't want to panic, but my alphabet soup says, "Forget about me; just try to save yourself."

Customer: “I can't find any chicken in the chicken soup.”

Waiter “Chef says you won't find any horse in the horseradish either."

Did you hear about the cross-eyed chef who got sacked because he couldn’t see eye to eye with his customers.

I got called pretty yesterday and it felt good. Actually, the full sentence was “You’re a pretty bad chef.” but I’m choosing to focus on the positive.

Yesterday, a chef's wife asked him to pass her lipstick but he passed her a super-glue stick instead by mistake. She still isn't talking to him.

A chef wanted to buy something nice for his boss, so he bought him a new chair. His boss won't let him plug it in though.

Truism – “Today's egg is better than tomorrow's hen."

Chapter 3: Question and Answer Chef Jokes

Q: What did the enthusiastic chef say to his staff?

A: Thyme flies when you're having fun.

Q: What is a chef's favourite type of music?

A: Wok 'n Roll.

Q: Why did the elderly chef retire?

A: His sage was showing.

Q: How many pastry chefs does it take to make a pie?

A: 3.14.

Q: Why don't pastry chefs buy tailor-made pastries?

A: Because they profiterole their own.

Q: What did the head chef say to chew out the new guy?

A: This steak is so undercooked that it's starting to eat the salad.

Q: What day of the week does a fish hate the most?

A: Fry-day.

Q: What happened when the chef crossed a chili pepper, a shovel and a labrador?

A: He got a hot-diggity-dog.

Q: Why did the chef get arrested for assault?

A: Because he was caught beating an egg.

Q: Why was the top chef's job in jeopardy?

A: His latest creation was a recipe for disaster.

Q: Why did the chef flip a pancake?

A: Because he was a tossed.

Q: What is a salad chef's favourite novel?

A: War and Peas.

Q: What is it called when a chef spills hot broth with dumplings onto a rude customer?

A: A Wonton Soup Attack.

Q: What does a pastry chef do at night?

A: He tells bread time stories.

Q: How do you know if an Italian chef loves you?

A: He steals a pizza your heart.

Q: What happens when you fall in love with a chef?

A: You will get buttered up.

Q: What is a chef's favourite dystopian movie?

A: The Hunger Games.

Q: Why did the finicky vegan chef quit?

A: Because they cut his celery.

Q: What did the Chef name his son?

A: Stew.

Q: What was the epileptic chef's house special?

A: Seizure salad.

Q: Why did the chef spill his soup?

A: Because there was a leek in the pot.

Q: What do you call a chef who is happy every Monday?

A: Retired.

Q: Did you hear about the Italian chef who died?

A: He pasta way.

Chapter 4: Short Chef Jokes

A chef went to a 24-hour grocery store to get some fresh vegetables.

Just as he got there, the guy was locking the front door.

The chef said, "Hey. The sign says you're open 24 hours."

The store owner replied, "Yes, but not in a row."

A young chef is in love with a girl and he goes to the girl's father to ask for her hand in marriage.

Her disapproving father says "With the money you earn, you can't even pay for my daughter's toilet paper."

The young chef replies, "Don't worry, I'm not going to marry a girl who is full of crap."

A guy sat down in a restaurant and ordered a bowl of mulligatawny soup.

"I'm sorry," the waitress said, "the chef does not recommend the soup, and anyway the customer next to you had the last bowl."

The guy could see that the other customer had left most of the soup.

"Could I have that?" he asked the other customer.

"Sure." he replied.

So he started eating--but halfway down he discovered a dead mouse.

"Ugh," he said, "I just found a dead mouse in the soup."

"That's as far as I got too," said the other man."

Two days ago, the chef's wife asked him to pass her lipstick but he passed her a stick of super-glue by mistake.

She still isn't talking to him.

A chef calls up his local paper and asks "How much would it be to put an ad in the paper?"

"Four dollars an inch," a woman replies. "Why? What are you selling?"

"A twenty eight inch high oven," said the chef before slamming the phone down.

Two chefs are having a conversation about sex. The first chef says that sex is 75% work and 25% pleasure. The second chef says that sex is 25% work and 75% pleasure. At a standstill, they decide to ask their sous chef's opinion.

“Sex is all pleasure” says the sous chef.

“Why do you say that?” ask the chefs.

To which the sous chef replies “Because if it there is any work involved, you two have me do it.”

A young junior chef is drinking at a bar one evening, when a big sweaty construction worker sits down next to him.

They get chatting, have a few more drinks and start to talk about Armageddon.

The chef asks the construction worker, "If you hear the sirens go off and you know you've got just twenty minutes left to live, just what would you do?"

The construction worker tells him, "I would try and make it with anything that moves."

The construction worker then asks the young chef what he would do to which he replies, "I would keep perfectly still."

A chef went to his boss and said, "I need a raise. Three other companies are after me."

He said, "Really? Which other companies are after you?"

The chef replied, "The electric company, the gas company and the water company."

Checking the menu, a restaurant customer ordered a bowl of vegetable soup.

After a couple spoonfuls, he saw a circle of wetness right under the bowl on the tablecloth.

He called the chef over and said, "It's all wet down here. The bowl must be cracked."

The chef said, "But you ordered the vegetable soup, didn't you?"

"Yes," he replied.

The chef tells him, "Well, maybe it has a leek in it."

The chef complained to his friend that his wife doesn't satisfy him anymore.

His friend suggested he finds another woman on the side, sharpish.

When they met up a month or so later, the chef told his friend "I took your advice. I managed to find a woman on the side, but my wife still doesn't satisfy me!"

A chef is out on safari and he catches a crocodile.

The crocodile tells him, "Please let me go. I'll grant you any wish you desire."

The chef says, "Okay, I wish my penis could touch the ground."

The crocodile then proceeds to bite the chef's legs off.

A chef is late for work and is struggling to find a parking space.

"Lord," he prayed. "I simply can't stand this. If you open up a space for me, I'll give up the booze and start to go to church every Sunday."

Suddenly, the clouds part and the sun shine on an empty parking spot.

Without hesitation, the chef says: "Never mind Lord, I found one."

A teacher asked his students to use the word "beans" in a sentence.

"My father grows beans," said the son of a farmer.

“My father cooks beans," said the son of a chef.

The son of a waiter spoke up, "We are all human beans."

A cannibal was walking through the jungle and came upon a restaurant opened by a fellow cannibal. Feeling somewhat hungry, he sat down and looked over the menu.

Roasted Explorer: $25.

Baked Missionary: $35.

Broiled Politician: $100.

The cannibal asked the chef, "Why such a price difference for the politician?

The chef replied "Have you ever tried to clean one of them?"

An 85 year old retired chef is walking through his local park and sees a frog.

He picks it up and the frog says to him, "If you kiss me, I will turn into a beautiful princess and make love to you every day for a whole year."

The old chef puts the frog in his pocket and the frog yells out "Didn't you hear what I said?"

The old chef looks at the frog and says, "Yes, but at my age I'd rather have a talking frog."

A chef thinks he is smart, but he is smug in his manner.

He told his chief waiter that an onion is the only food that makes you cry, so the waiter threw a coconut at his face.

The chef is not so smug now.

A boy is selling fish on a street corner and to get people’s attention, he is shouting, "Dam fish for sale. Get your dam fish here."

A chef hears this and asks, "Why are you calling them 'dam fish.'" to which the boy replies, "Because I caught these fish at the local dam."

The junior chef buys a couple of fish, takes them to the restaurant and asks the chef how to cook dam fish.

The chef is surprised at his language. Later as the junior chef is plating up a meal, the chef says “Hurry up with the dam fish.”

The junior chef responds, "It’s on its way, I just need to finish cooking the f*cking potatoes."

A man walked into a restaurant and said, "I'd like a bowl of soup and a kind word.”

The waiter brought his soup a few minutes later.

As he put it down, the man whispered, "How about the kind word?"

The waiter said, "Don't eat the soup."

A wealthy man came home from a disastrous gambling trip and told his wife that he had lost their entire fortune and that they would have to drastically alter their lavish life-style.

"If you'll just learn to cook," he said, "we can fire the chef."

"Okay," the wife said. "And if you learn how to make love properly, then we can fire the gardener too."

A chef goes to the doctor with a hearing problem.

The doctor says, “Can you describe the symptoms to me?”

The chef replies, “Yes. Homer is a fat yellow lazy man and his wife Marge is skinny with big blue hair.”

A chef with a monkey on his shoulder was walking down the road when he passed a policeman who said, "I think you had better take that monkey to the zoo."

The next day, the chef was walking down the road with the monkey on his shoulder again, when he passed the same policeman.

The policeman said, "Hey, I thought I told you to take that monkey to the zoo."

The chef answered, "I did; and today I'm taking him to the cinema."

A chef meets up with his blonde girlfriend as she's picking up her car from the mechanic.

"Everything ok with your car now?" he asks.

"Yes, thank goodness," the dipsy blonde replies.

"Weren't you worried the mechanic might try to rip you off?"

"Yes, but he didn't. I was so relieved when he told me that all I needed was blinker fluid!"

A chef cooks a deer for dinner at home.

Both he and his wife decide that they won't tell the kids what kind of meat it is, but will give them a clue and let them guess.

The chef tells his kids, "It's what Mommy calls me sometimes."

The little girl screams to her brother, "Don't eat it. It’s an a**hole.

Chapter 5: Longer Chef Jokes

Chefs Prayer

Two chefs are walking through a game park and they come across a lion that has not eaten for days.

The lion starts chasing the two men.

They run as fast as they can and one of the chefs tires and decides to say a prayer, "Please turn this lion into a Christian, Lord."

He looks around to see if the lion is still chasing and he sees the lion on its knees.

Happy to see his prayer answered, he turns around and walks towards the lion.

As he gets closer to the lion, he hears the lion saying a prayer: "Thank you Lord for the food I am about to receive."

Train Passengers

A chef, an attorney, a beautiful lady, and an old woman were all on a train, sitting 2x2 facing each other.

The train went into a tunnel and when the carriage went completely dark, a "thwack" was heard. When the train came back out of the tunnel into the light the attorney had a red hand print where he had been slapped on the face.

The old lady thought, "That attorney must have groped the young lady in the dark and she slapped him."

The hottie thought, "That attorney must have tried to grope me, got the old lady by mistake, and she slapped him."

The attorney thought, "That chef must have groped the hottie, she thought it was me, and slapped me."

The chef sat there thinking, "I can't wait for another tunnel so I can slap that horrible attorney again."

Minced Beef

A guy orders a hamburger in a diner, and the waiter puts the order through.

The kitchen is on display to everyone and the customers sees the chef take a large piece of minced beef, screw it into a ball, and place the ball of meat into the ball of his armpit, and then proceed to pump his arm several times to squeeze the meat flat.

He then puts the flattened meat onto the grill to cook it.

"That's the most nauseating piece of food preparation I have ever seen," says the customer, to which the waiter replies “You think that’s bad? Well, you really don’t want to see him make doughnuts."

Trucker’s Slang

A young waiter in a diner has a trucker sit down and order, "Gimme three flat tires and a couple of headlights."

Bewildered, he goes to the kitchen and tells the chef, "I think this guy's in the wrong store, look at what he ordered."

The chef says, "It’s slang. He wants three pancakes and two eggs sunny-side up."

The waiter takes a bowl of beans to the trucker.

The trucker looks at it and grumbles, "What's this? I didn't order this."

The young man tells him, "The chef says that while you're waiting for your parts, you might as well gas up."

Chef's Wife

A chef suspected his wife was cheating on him.

He explained his situation to a pet shop owner who replied, "I have a parrot that will let you know what goes on in your house every day.

The bird has no legs, so he holds onto his perch with his penis."

Reluctantly, the chef bought the bird and took him home.

At the end of the first day, the chef asked the bird, "Did anything happen today?"

The parrot said, "Yes, the milk man came over."

The chef asked, "What happened?"

The bird said, "They both took their clothes off."

“Then what happened?” said the chef to which the parrot replied “I don’t know; I got hard and fell off my perch.”

Free Drink

A chef walks into a bar and the bartender says, "If you can make that horse over there laugh, you can get free drinks for the rest of the night."

The chef walks over, says something to the horse, it laughs, and he walks back over to the bar to collect his free drinks.

The next night, the chef goes back to the bar and the bartender asks the chef if he can make the horse cry.

The man walks over, does something to the horse, and it starts to cry.

The bartender asks, "How did you make it cry?"

The chef replies, "Well, to make the horse laugh last night I told it I had a bigger dick and to make it cry tonight I showed it."

Reunion

A group of chefs, all aged 40, discussed where they should meet for a reunion lunch. They agreed they would meet at a place called The Dog House because the barmaids had big breasts and wore short-skirts.

Ten years later, the chefs, now aged 50, once again discussed where they should meet for lunch.

It was agreed that they should meet at The Dog House because the food and service was good and there was an excellent beer selection.

Ten years later, the chefs now aged 60, discussed where they should meet for lunch.

It was agreed that they should meet at The Dog House because there were plenty of parking spaces, they could dine in peace and quiet, and it was good value for money.

Ten years later, the chefs now aged 70, discussed where they should meet for lunch.

It was agreed that they should meet at The Dog House because the restaurant was wheelchair accessible and had a toilet for the disabled.

Ten years later, the retired chefs, now aged 80, discussed where they should meet for lunch.

Finally it was agreed that they should meet at The Dog House because they had never been there before.

Crazy Chef

A chef goes to a busy bar with an alligator. He says to the crowd, "I bet you that I can put my dick into this alligator's mouth for ten seconds, and when I take it out, it will not be damaged."

He continued, "If I succeed, all of you will buy me a drink. If I fail, I will buy all of you a drink."

The other men agree to the deal and so the chef puts his dick into the alligator's mouth and the alligator closes its mouth.

Ten seconds later, he hits the alligator on the head with a beer bottle, and the alligator opens his mouth.

To everyone's surprise, the chef's dick is unharmed. "Now, before you buy me drinks, does anybody else want to try?"

After a while, a woman raises her hand.

"I will try," she says, "but you have to promise not to hit me on the head so hard."

Three Daughters

A male chef was talking to two of his friends about their teenage daughters.

The first friend says "I was cleaning my daughter's room the other day and I found a pack of cigarettes. I didn't even know she smoked."

The second friend says, "That's nothing. I was cleaning my daughter's room the other day and I found a half full bottle of gin. I didn't even know she drank."

The chef says, "That's nothing. I was cleaning my daughter's room the other day and I found a pack of condoms. I didn't even know she had a penis."

Talking Parrot

A chef buys a talking parrot from a pet shop.

He takes the parrot home and tries to teach the parrot how to say a few things, but instead, the parrot just swears at him.

After a few hours of trying to teach the bird, the chef finally says, "If you don't stop swearing, I'm going to put you in the freezer as punishment."

The parrot continues, so the chef puts the bird in the freezer.

About an hour later, the parrot pleads with the chef to open the door.

As the chef takes the shivering bird out of the freezer, it says, "I promise to never swear again. Just tell me what that turkey did."

Cannibals

A Frenchman, an Englishman and a New Yorker were captured by cannibals. The chief comes to them and says, "The bad news is that we're going to kill you. We will put you in a pot, cook you, eat you and then we're going to use your skins to build a canoe. The good news is that you can choose how to die."

The Frenchman says, "I take ze sword." The chief gives him a sword, the Frenchman says, "Vive La France." and runs himself through.

The Englishman says, "I will have a pistol please." The chief gives him a pistol, the Englishman points it at his head and says, "God save the Queen." and proceeds to blow his brains out.

The New Yorker says, "Gimme a fork." The chief gives him a fork. The New Yorker takes the fork and starts jabbing himself all over- the stomach, the sides, the chest, all over his body, with blood gushing out everywhere. The chief yells, "What are you doing?"

The New Yorker responds, "So much for your canoe, you dumb cannibal."

Chef's Affair

A married chef was having an affair with a waitress.

One day, their passions overcame them in the kitchen and they went back to her house.

Exhausted from the afternoon's activities, they fell asleep and eventually awoke at about 8pm.

As the chef put on his clothes, he told the waitress to take his shoes outside and rub them through the grass and dirt.

Confused, she did as she was asked, and the chef then out his shoes on and drove home.

"Where have you been?" demanded the chef's wife when he entered the house.

"Darling," replied the chef, "I can't lie to you. I've been having an affair with a waitress. I fell asleep in her bed and didn't wake up until half an hour or so ago."

The wife looked down at his shoes and said, "You liar. You've been playing golf."'

A Couple Of Eggs

A drunk staggers into a diner and orders some scrambled eggs on toast. The waiter, suspecting that they've run out of eggs queries it with the chef who replies, "I ran out of fresh eggs earlier, I just have two rotten eggs at the back of the fridge."

The waiter says, "Cook up the rotten eggs. He is so drunk he won't be able to tell the difference."

The chef scrambles up the rotten eggs and heaps the mix onto some toast.

The drunk is hungry and he gobbles up the food without saying anything.

He is ready to pay and asks the waiter, "Just where did you get those eggs from?"

The waiter replies, "We have our own chicken farm out back."

The drunk asks, "Do you have a rooster?

"No," says the waiter.

"Well, I suggest you get one”, says the drunk, “because I think a skunk is screwing your chickens."

Chapter 6: Chef Pick Up Lines

I have a delicious job. I'm a chef.

I would love to check out your mixing bowl.

Your skin is smoother than the finest panna cotta.

Dinner is on me. I know the chef.

Staring at you is better than looking at food porn.

You're twice as sweet as a creme brulee, and a lot less drippy.

You’re finer than my pepper.

I can do amazing things to your tongue.

Once the rainy season arrives, we should forage together.

I want to flush your pipes, baby.

Want to see my meat walk-in?

Have I got a bone for you.

If I was a watermelon, would you spit or swallow my seed?

Need your knife sharpened, baby?

You make me smoking hot, like 220 degrees all day.

You make my highly sensitive palate water.

You dance like a headless chicken. I can't wait to pick your feathers.

Chapter 7: Bumper Stickers For Chefs

Chemistry is like Cooking.

I don’t cook - I create!

Real men don’t use recipes.

Note to self: When washing chef’s coat always check pockets.

Life is too short to stuff a mushroom.

Hey, that's pretty well it for this book. I hope you've enjoyed it.

I've written a few other joke books for other professions, and here are just a few from my electricians joke book:-

Q: What kind of van does an electrician drive?

A: A *Volts-wagon.*

Q: What do you call a Russian electrician?

A: *Switchitonanov.*

Q: What is the definition of a shock absorber?

A: *A careless electrician.*

About the Author

Chester Croker has written many joke books and was named Comedy Writer Of The Year by the International Jokers Guild. Chester, known to his friends as Chester the Jester, just loves cooking which has provided him with plenty of material for this joke book.

If you see anything wrong, or you have a gag you would like to see included in the next edition of this book, please do so via the glowwormpress.com website.

If you did enjoy the book, kindly leave a review on Amazon so that other chefs can have a good laugh too.

Thanks in advance.

Printed by Amazon Italia Logistica S.r.l.
Torrazza Piemonte (TO), Italy